LORD
BALTIMORE
FOUNDER OF MARYLAND

SPECIAL LIVES IN HISTORY THAT BECOME

Signature LIVES

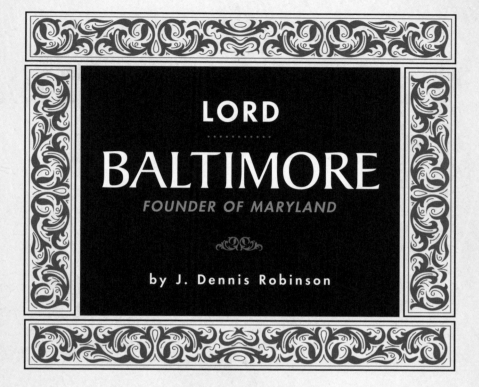

LORD
BALTIMORE
FOUNDER OF MARYLAND

by J. Dennis Robinson

Content Adviser: Silas Hurry, Curator of Collections,
Department of Research and Collections,
Historic St. Mary's City, Maryland

Reading Adviser: Susan Kesselring, M.A.,
Literacy Educator, Rosemount–Apple Valley–Eagan
(Minnesota) School District

COMPASS POINT BOOKS ✦ MINNEAPOLIS, MINNESOTA

Compass Point Books
3109 West 50th Street, #115
Minneapolis, MN 55410

Visit Compass Point Books on the Internet at *www.compasspointbooks.com*
or e-mail your request to *custserv@compasspointbooks.com*

Editor: Nick Healy
Page Production: The Design Lab
Photo Researcher: Svetlana Zhurkin
Cartographer: XNR Productions, Inc.
Library Consultant: Kathleen Baxter

Art Director: Jaime Martens
Creative Director: Keith Griffin
Editorial Director: Carol Jones
Managing Editor: Catherine Neitge

Library of Congress Cataloging-in-Publication Data
Robinson, J. Dennis.
  Lord Baltimore : founder of Maryland / by J. Dennis Robinson.
     p. cm. — (Signature lives)
  Includes bibliographical references and index.
  ISBN 0-7565-1592-0 (hard cover)
  1. Baltimore, Cecil Calvert, Baron, ca. 1605-1675—Juvenile literature.
2. Calvert family—Juvenile literature. 3. Maryland—History—Colonial
period, ca. 1600-1775—Biography—Juvenile literature. 4. Maryland—
History—Colonial period, ca. 1600-1775—Juvenile literature. I. Title. II.
Series.
  F184.R63 2006
  975.2'02—dc22   2005027112

Signature Lives

COLONIAL AMERICA

As they arrived in North America, European colonists found an expansive land of potential riches and unlimited opportunities. Many left their homes in the Old World seeking religious and political freedom. Others sought the chance to build a better life for themselves. The effort to settle a vast new land was not easy, and the colonists faced struggles over land, religion, and freedoms. But despite the many conflicts, great cities emerged, new industries developed, and the foundation for a new type of government was laid. Meanwhile, Native Americans fought to keep their ancestral lands and traditions alive in a rapidly changing world that became as new to them as it was to the colonists.

Table of Contents

1 VOYAGE TO MARYLAND

ᕦᕤ

The weather was ideal for sailing when the *Ark* and *Dove* left England on November 22, 1633. One hundred and forty passengers waved farewell to friends at the port of Cowes as the two heavily laden wooden ships slipped away from the Isle of Wight on a soft southeastern breeze. Their long journey to begin a new colony in the wilderness of America was safely under way—or so it seemed.

Cecil Calvert, the young founder of Maryland and better known as Lord Baltimore, had a bold idea. He was determined to create a profitable colony run by both Catholics and Protestants. This had never been done. Catholics in England during Lord Baltimore's lifetime were often persecuted for their beliefs. Even with the title of Lord Baltimore,

Cecil Calvert was the second Lord Baltimore and the founder of the Maryland Colony.

he had to downplay the fact that he was a Catholic. By sending a party to Maryland and creating a successful British colony, Lord Baltimore hoped to prove his loyalty to the king and to rule his own land—a more tolerant one.

But Lord Baltimore was not aboard either of the boats that day. The *Ark* and *Dove* sailed without him, and for good reason. Although he is remembered as a thoughtful and wise man, Lord Baltimore had enemies. If he joined the colonists in America, he feared, powerful people who wanted to see his colony fail might convince King Charles I to take back the land he had granted to the Calvert family. Someone had to stay in England to defend his rights to the land.

Maryland colonists sailed aboard the Ark *and* Dove.

So at the last moment, Lord Baltimore sent his younger brother to Maryland in his place. As colonial governor, Leonard Calvert's job was to follow his brother's instructions and to report back regularly. In the 1600s, it took months to send a letter across the Atlantic Ocean and to get a reply, and once a ship left port, it was out of touch until it reached land again.

Lord Baltimore had no way of knowing what his colonists faced in their early days at sea. A sudden storm arose, with hurricane-force winds that hammered the two ships as they rolled helplessly among crushing waves. Except for those able-bodied men who could assist the frantic crew, Lord Baltimore's colonists clung to one another below deck in the belly of the *Ark*, praying for their lives. They had lost track of the *Dove*. The smaller ship had disappeared during the second day out of port. One moment its two signal fires were dimly visible through the driving rain, but a moment later the *Dove* was gone.

The worst came in the dark of night. The captain screamed against the rising wind, commanding

> *The first Maryland colonists traveled from England in two ships that seem to have taken their names—the* Ark *and* Dove—*from the biblical tale of Noah. In the Old Testament story, Noah built a massive wooden ark. Only the animals and people aboard survived a flood that drowned all other life on Earth. Noah knew the flood was over when a small dove he sent out returned carrying a green twig.*

the men to haul in every sail or else the *Ark* would certainly capsize. Only the main sail was still aloft when the powerful wind struck, tearing the sail from top to bottom and flinging half the precious canvas into the sea.

Many onboard abandoned all hope. They knew Captain John Smith's expedition had met a similar fate just a decade before. Smith, the hero of Jamestown, Virginia, had hoped to found his own colony in New England when suddenly his expedition was caught in a hellish storm. His ships, Smith later wrote, were damaged beyond repair, and surviving colonists gave up and returned home.

Father Andrew White, who recorded the harrowing tale of the *Ark*, wrote that the ship was as helpless as a dish on the water. It was, he wrote, as if "all the mischievous storm spirits and evil genii of Maryland had appeared in battle line against us."

Yet by morning, the sea had calmed, and it remained welcoming for the rest of the three-month voyage. The frightened colonists, both Catholics and Protestants, who had prayed so desperately for their survival the night before, now came to believe that their journey was blessed by a higher power. They quickly repaired the *Ark*, and Leonard instructed the captain to set a course for the West Indies.

Six weeks later, the crew and passengers of the *Ark* found themselves in the Caribbean Sea, stopping on island shores and soaking up the tropical sun. By some miracle or by "divine providence," they believed, passengers of the *Ark* had escaped being adrift without wind and tortured by relentless heat, like many earlier travelers. White's journal, in which he reported back to Lord Baltimore, is filled with details of colorful birds, exotic plants, and native customs. The Caribbean was a world of lushness and abundance. After weeks of eating dried beef, hard biscuits, and salted fish, the colonists were nearly intoxicated by the flavors of papaya, guava, and coconut. White struggled to describe the flavor of pineapples, which he told Lord Baltimore was like no other in the world: "It has an aromatic taste, which I would say resembles strawberries mixed with wine and sugar."

Much of what is known about the first Maryland colonists comes from the eyewitness account made by a Roman Catholic priest. Father Andrew White (1579-1656) was in his 50s during the dangerous voyage. His mission was to tell the Native Americans about his religion in hopes of converting them to Christianity. His report offers a behind-the-scenes look at the founding of one of the original American colonies. White wrote his report in the ancient language of Latin, which was used by scholars and the Catholic Church.

The colonists dallied for a month in the Caribbean, according to White. Although around a dozen of them became sick with fever and died, most escaped the illnesses commonly suffered by tropical travelers. While there, the colonists grew healthier in preparation for the difficult task ahead in Maryland.

Amazingly, the *Ark* reunited with the *Dove*, which had not sunk after all. The pinnace—the term used to describe small sailing ships—had instead turned back to England to avoid the rising storm, then set sail again. In the eyes of the Maryland colonists, their journey to America had been doubly blessed.

And their good fortune held. The *Ark* and *Dove* hopped safely from one Caribbean island to the next and then sailed to the eastern coast of colonial America. Their goal was the Chesapeake, a bay stretching 200 miles (320 kilometers) long with shores along modern-day Maryland and Virginia. In early March, after pausing for several days in Virginia, Lord Baltimore's colonists sailed farther into the beautiful Chesapeake Bay—deep, wide, circled by fertile soil and tall trees, and teeming with fish. The forests were filled with game. The local Indians, for the most part, were generous and helpful. In thanks, the group raised a large wooden cross on Maryland's St. Clement's Island and celebrated their first Catholic Mass in America.

The Maryland Colony was, from the start, a sort of paradise. Previous settlers in North America had not found such comforts. Many of the early Virginians had starved to death or been killed by Indians. The Puritans in Massachusetts had barely survived their first winter.

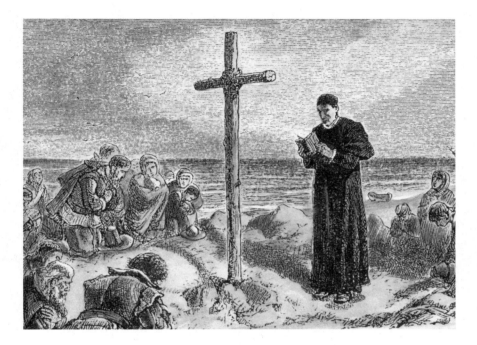

But Lord Baltimore had learned from history. Although he stayed back in England, his careful planning got the Marylanders off to a successful start.

Newly arrived in Maryland, the settlers celebrated the first Catholic Mass in the English colonies.

The group arrived at the beginning of the planting season with plenty of seeds and all the right tools. The step-by-step instructions they followed came from Lord Baltimore himself, the man who, according to British law, owned all the land in the Maryland grant. Back in England, after tense weeks waiting for a letter, Maryland's founder and patron learned about the harrowing storm and received the news of the amazing journey. Lord Baltimore's dream—a dream inherited from his father—was coming true. 🕭

2 THE LORDS BALTIMORE

❧❀❧

Cecil Calvert, the oldest of 11 children, was born into privilege in 1605 in Kent, England. His father, George Calvert, had just begun a rapid climb up the English social ladder when Cecil was born. Cecil's mother, Anne Mynne, was from a wealthy Catholic family and, like her husband, had to balance her faith with her public life. These two factors—wealth and religion—would shape Cecil's childhood and his adult life.

Wealth and property had not come easily to Cecil's father. Born around 1578, George Calvert was the son of a Yorkshire landholder and cattle farmer. The family name *Calvert* may have evolved, over generations, from the words "calf herd." While his parents were by no means poor, their social status was far below the wealthy nobility who ruled England. Worse, George's

George Calvert, the first Lord Baltimore, rose from modest beginnings to a position of power in the British government.

parents were Roman Catholics, members of a faith that was banned under the reign of Queen Elizabeth I. To protect their family from possible arrest, even death, George's parents gave up their faith. They reluctantly converted—on the surface, at least—to the Church of England and sent George to Protestant schools.

At age 14, George was able to attend Trinity College at Oxford University, one of the most prestigious schools in the country. His son Cecil would later attend the same school. An excellent student, George rubbed elbows with young gentlemen from the finest families. Especially good with languages, he graduated from college at 17. His long climb up the social ladder began almost immediately, when he became an assistant secretary to Lord Robert Cecil, the powerful earl of Salisbury. Lord Cecil was also secretary of state to King James I and his predecessor, Queen Elizabeth.

George was a practical man, as his son Cecil would later prove to be. George knew that the only way to survive and thrive in the monarchy was to please powerful people. He worked very hard for Lord Cecil who, in turn, worked to please the king. George also married well, choosing in Anne Mynne a woman whose family was rich and influential. The couple named their first child Cecil Calvert, in honor of Lord Robert Cecil.

As the oldest son of an important man, Cecil was required to conduct himself with poise and dignity. The more Cecil's father gained wealth and status by working for the king, the more he was required to travel and spend time away from his family. And Cecil's mother was often ill, which meant that even as a child Cecil had a great deal of responsibility.

Cecil's father had made his way to the core of power with surprising speed. He became clerk of the Privy Council, the inner circle of England's government, and had direct access to the king. For his loyalty and good work, George was knighted by the king in 1617. This officially made him a member of the British upper class. Two years later, George replaced his mentor, Lord Cecil, as secretary of state,

King Henry VIII started the split between the Protestant and Catholic churches in England in 1533. Henry wanted to divorce his first wife because she did not give birth to a son and heir. But Henry was a Roman Catholic and his religion did not allow divorce. So Henry broke away from the Catholic pope in Rome and started his own Protestant religion. Henry eventually had six wives, but only one son, Edward, who outlived him by only five years.

a job that required George to represent the king in matters of foreign policy. He was now the right-hand man of one of the most powerful people in Europe.

But Cecil's father had a dangerous secret—his religious faith. In England, the king was the leader of the Protestant church, which was run by the government. Yet in his heart, George was a Roman Catholic and not a Protestant. In 1625, King James died, and King Charles, who took a harsher stand against Catholics, took over the throne. George then openly announced that he was a Catholic and resigned his post on the Privy Council.

It was a risky political move, but Sir George Calvert was a practical and ambitious man. He guessed that his long service to the crown had earned him trust in return. He was right. King Charles, whose own wife came from a Catholic family, made him the baron of Baltimore, a noble title that included a large manor farm in Ireland. George Calvert would be known as the first Lord Baltimore, and his son Cecil would later become the second.

George boldly suggested to the king that he could serve England in a new and exciting way by founding a British colony in the New World. George was fascinated by America. It was a land of adventure— and of great potential wealth and a new level of religious freedom. Each early American colony was backed by businessmen, who risked their money in

King Charles (seated) presented a charter for Avalon, New Foundland, to the first Lord Baltimore.

hopes of earning a profit off the crops and the land. George had already been among the investors in the Virginia Company, an experimental American colony founded at Jamestown in 1607, when Cecil was still an infant. In 1620, when Cecil was a teenager, his father had invested in the New England Company that supported a group, later known as the Pilgrims, settling at Plymouth, Massachusetts.

Then in 1621, George joined the investors in a colonial enterprise on the island of Newfoundland, part of present-day Canada. Though he stayed in England, George sent colonists to Ferryland, in the extreme eastern end of the island. At a place that would be known as Avalon, the colonists created a small fishing settlement.

Then in 1622, tragedy struck the Calvert family when Anne Mynne, Cecil's mother, died. Cecil was a teenager and saw his father become extremely saddened. George had once described his wife as "the dear companion and only comfort of my life." As the oldest of the Calvert children, Cecil knew that a great deal of family responsibility rested on his shoulders.

In those days, the oldest son usually followed in his father's footsteps in work and in life. Cecil lived much of his young life in his father's grand home named Kiplin Hall in Yorkshire, and for a time stayed in a rented home in London. From early on, Cecil learned to manage affairs at home when his father was away. Also from an early age, Cecil apparently shared his father's passion for the mysterious and exciting New World across the Atlantic Ocean.

Several important changes affected the Calvert family in the years after Cecil's mother died. In the late 1620s, Cecil married Anne Arundell, and the first of the couple's five children was born soon thereafter. Anne was the daughter of a British nobleman, who gave the couple land in Wiltshire, where they would live in a home called Hook House. Marriage had only increased Cecil's wealth and land holdings.

Cecil's father, meanwhile, became increasingly determined to make his mark on history. George told

King Charles of England distrusted Roman Catholics but granted the Calverts their colonies.

King Charles that he wanted to go to Avalon himself and build up that colony. All George wanted was one more royal gift—a charter from the king granting him the land. The king agreed, and the Avalon Colony was officially chartered to the Calvert family forever.

In 1627, having resigned his positions in government and embracing his Catholic faith,

George sailed to Newfoundland to visit his new colony. Cecil stayed behind in England. In Avalon, George would be like the king of his own country, with the right to make his own laws, assign land, and collect taxes. The charter from King Charles gave George all of those powers. He owed the king only his loyalty and a portion of any gold or silver discovered in the colony.

George's kingdom, however, turned out to be nothing but a crude fishing outpost. All the settlers were gone, and the colony was abandoned. But George still had hope. With hard work and new settlers, he imagined, Avalon would become not only a profitable colony, but also a safe haven for Catholics like himself.

After only a short visit at the height of summer, George rushed back to England to make further arrangements. Although he heard reports that the Canadian winters were long and cold, George did not take the warnings seriously. He was determined to get back to the New World. By this time, he had remarried and wanted to share his adventure. George brought his new wife, Joan, and most of his children on the next ship across the Atlantic to their new home in Avalon. Cecil's brother Leonard, who would later play an important role in the Maryland Colony, traveled with his father, but Cecil again remained in England to manage the family estates. It was a role Cecil would

The Avalon Colony's forge, where metal was heated and shaped

play throughout the rest of his life.

The move to Canada was George's first great mistake. The killing cold of the Newfoundland winter was more than his family could bear. Before long, he sent his children back to England, while George and his wife stayed on.

The frigid days and howling winds, George wrote, made it nearly impossible even to breathe. His house became a hospital where 100 colonists huddled in the cold, half of them sick and dying. George himself was very ill and scarcely survived the winter. But he did not easily abandon his dream of a profitable colony open to both Protestants and Catholics.

Maryland Colony, 1632
Map shows present-day state and country boundaries.

Ferryland (Avalon Colony)

ASIA
NORTH AMERICA
Caribbean Sea
ATLANTIC OCEAN
AFRICA

CANADA

N
W E
S

0   200 miles
0   200 kilometers

UNITED STATES

Atlantic Ocean

St. Mary's

Chesapeake Bay

North Sea
Atlantic Ocean
UNITED KINGDOM
IRELAND Yorkshire
London

After winter struggles in the Avalon Colony, the Calverts created the Maryland Colony to the south.

Finally, after one winter in Newfoundland, George left Avalon in disappointment. He took his wife and the surviving settlers on a ship bound for Virginia. Even before leaving, he had petitioned King Charles for one more royal favor. George wanted a different grant of land.

The region south of the Virginia Colony looked promising for settlement, but the Virginians were already expanding into the area. However, there was a perfect spot between Virginia and the colonies to the northeast. George proposed calling it Crescentia, but King Charles had a better idea. The odd-shaped space should be called Maria's Land, after the king's wife, Queen Henrietta Maria. The name they eventually agreed upon was Maryland.

The Virginians did not want a Catholic like George around. Some were afraid he might ask the king to grant him control of Virginia, so they demanded George take an oath expressing his loyalty and providing them reassurance. But George believed the oath was something his Catholic faith would not allow. Instead, he left his wife behind and returned to England to negotiate the terms of his charter for Maryland with the king.

The Maryland Colony was named after Queen Henrietta Maria.

Then the first Lord Baltimore suffered his second tragedy. In 1630, he sent for his wife and servants. They left the American colonies and sailed for England, but their ship crashed against the rocks within sight of the English shore. All the people aboard were lost. Again George was overcome with sadness, and again he threw himself into his plans for starting his own American colony.

Kiplin Hall, once the Calvert home in Yorkshire, England

Although he had lost a lot of money in his colony at Avalon, George continued to press the king to grant him a second charter, this one giving him control of Maryland. Virginia colonists protested Calvert's request for land that they considered part of their own colony. To be closer to the seat of government, George moved back to London, where he could urge the king to approve his request. George arrived just as the city was suffering a deadly attack of the plague, a disease that killed thousands.

The political process moved slowly, and by now, George was not healthy, possibly weakened by the illness he had suffered during his frigid winter at Avalon. On April 15, 1632, George Calvert died while waiting for his land grant to receive royal approval. He missed hearing the good news by just two months. On June 20, 1632, the Charter of Maryland became official. It passed immediately to George's son Cecil.

Cecil Calvert inherited his father's fortune, his land, and his destiny. The death of his father also officially gave Cecil the title Lord Baltimore and the responsibility to oversee a large barony—a private estate—in Ireland. Cecil, at age 27, also inherited his father's mansion and sprawling farm in Yorkshire, England. And as heir of the Charter of Maryland, Cecil inherited 12 million acres (4.8 million hectares) of land in America.

His father had dreamed of building a colony there—3,000 miles (4,800 km) away in the rich black soil along the Chesapeake Bay. As the second Lord Baltimore, Cecil would also spend much of his life planning, nurturing, and fretting over that distant colony, but he would never see it. 🍂

3 TAKING THE LEAD

Chapter

❧❧❧

The early steps of building the Maryland Colony centered on preparations made in England. Although he never held public office like his father, the new Lord Baltimore was clearly an effective salesman and politician. Using printed pamphlets, similar to modern-day travel brochures, he was able to convince people to risk their lives and their money to help start his colony.

Little is known of Lord Baltimore's daily life at the time, but historians have gathered details about him from his actions. Sending off his colonists, Lord Baltimore proved an expert planner. He organized the expedition right down to determining the amount of food and drink aboard the *Ark*, which sailed with provisions that included 107 tons of beer.

As Lord Baltimore, Cecil Calvert led preparations to send his colonists on the journey to America.

The Maryland Charter offered a detailed list of exactly what Lord Baltimore owned in his new colony. The proprietor could claim, for example, all ports, harbors, bays, rivers, straits, or islands. He owned the soil, plains, woods, marshes, and lakes within his boundaries. In the water, he owned all "whales, sturgeon and other royal fish." The king, however, wanted a share of any gold, silver, gems, and precious stones "or any other thing or matter whatsoever." English colonial investors like George Calvert had high hopes of discovering natural riches in the New World, but were continually disappointed.

Lord Baltimore specified how much of everything was needed for passengers, including specific quantities of vinegar, salt, fruit, and meat. He told colonists what to bring, including their bedding, tools, clothes, equipment, and supplies. He wanted to control every tiny aspect of the Maryland Colony from his home base far away in England. His original instructions to the colonists also offered directions for planting crops, designing the town, making gardens, training the military, dealing with Indians, and more.

He was also cautious, telling younger brother Leonard to be wary of possible enemies in North America. Also, he was concerned about religion, working with his Catholic missionaries to convince the American Indians to become Christians while at the same time attempting to further religious tolerance in Maryland. Finally, Lord Baltimore believed in fairness, instructing his brother to be careful to "do justice to every man without partiality."

Lord Baltimore sent the two boats—the *Ark* and *Dove*—across the Atlantic Ocean with the settlers bound for Maryland. Leonard traveled aboard one of the ships and represented his brother as the leader of the mission. In his written instructions to Leonard, Lord Baltimore warned that the Catholics aboard the *Ark* must keep a low profile when practicing their religious traditions. He did not want them to anger or offend the Protestants aboard the ship. Lord Baltimore lived his own life by the same rule. He attracted very little attention in England, and he was careful about displaying his religious faith. He did not want to give anyone a reason to dislike or distrust him.

Leonard Calvert was the first governor of the Maryland Colony.

Lord Baltimore did not want to stay behind in England, but he could not take the chance that his enemies might convince the king to withdraw the Maryland charter. In the written instructions given to Leonard in 1633, Lord Baltimore asked his brother to tell the colonists that he "hath deferred his owne

William Claiborne's trading post on Kent Island, shown in a 19th-century illustration, was included in the Maryland Charter.

coming till the next yeare, when he will not faile by the grace of god to be there." But Lord Baltimore would not come. Crisis after crisis forced him to stay close to London to protect his colony and his legal control over it. By remaining in England, he kept his American colony alive.

The problems in the English court began before the colonists even sailed. A group of Virginia planters presented their case against Lord Baltimore in writing to the Privy Council in June 1632. Parts of the planned Maryland colony had already been settled by Virginians, they said. Virginian William Claiborne, who would become a longtime foe of Lord Baltimore's Maryland, had set up a profitable fur trading post on Kent Island, which was now included in Lord Baltimore's land charter.

The Virginians, including Claiborne, tried every argument they could imagine to prevent the Calverts from owning Maryland. They complained to the council that Lord Baltimore was a subversive who was planning to set up a Catholic colony in the New World and join with the Spanish to attack England. They argued that Catholics were plotting to spread their religion in America.

> *William Claiborne (c. 1600–1677) was Lord Baltimore's most persistent foe. The son of an English gentleman from Kent, Claiborne served as an officer in the army of volunteer soldiers defending Jamestown in 1621. Claiborne was also a surveyor—measuring and mapping land for the London Company and battling Indians in Virginia. In thanks for his service to Virginia, the government gave him a piece of land on the eastern side of Chesapeake Bay, where he set up a profitable trading post at Kent Island.*

This legal attack could have been the end of the Maryland plan. However, the Privy Council had long been friendly with the Calvert family. Also, Lord Baltimore's well-written legal defense impressed the council members. His arguments and influence were more powerful than those of his Virginian opponents. His paper titled "Objectives Answered Touching Maryland" finally convinced the council that his colony would expand, not damage, the growing British Empire. The Privy Council decided in his favor. Claiborne and other Virginians, the council said, had no right to petition the king about land that had clearly been given to Lord Baltimore.

The dispute slowed the start of the voyage and depleted Lord Baltimore's dwindling fortune. And the attacks he endured only convinced him further that someone had to stay behind to fight for Maryland at the English court. When the *Ark* and *Dove* finally sailed in November 1633, Lord Baltimore wrote to a friend, "I have at last sent away my ships, and have deferred my going until another time."

After surviving the perilous storm that separated the ships and nearly claimed both, the settlers sailed into the calm Caribbean Sea. They had spent six weeks crossing the Atlantic Ocean, and after the difficult trip, they passed a month recuperating in the warm, calm Caribbean. When the boats aimed north again, the settlers were at last headed for their final destination.

Lord Baltimore had warned his brother to steer clear of Virginia when his boats arrived in North America. But Leonard decided to meet his new neighbors face-to-face. When the travel-weary

The wind-swept entrance to Chesapeake Bay from the waters of the Atlantic Ocean

settlers stopped at Point Comfort, Virginia, most of the Virginians there welcomed them. The settlers stayed briefly in Virginia before moving farther into Chesapeake Bay and finally setting foot on Maryland soil, where settlers celebrated their famous first Catholic Mass in the American colonies.

Lord Baltimore had won the first round in his fight to build an American colony, and his vision was becoming a reality. However, Claiborne and other Protestant enemies of the Maryland Colony had just begun to fight. And the Virginians were not the only foes of Lord Baltimore's new colony. ✍

Chapter
4 GROWING HIS COLONY

७∞৩

Who owned the New World? For the early European colonists, the answer was simple: whoever got there first. With Spanish settlements to the south of his holdings and French settlements to the north, King Charles wanted to quickly stake out as much British land as possible along the middle Atlantic coast of North America. Lord Baltimore's land grant in Maryland neatly filled in a gap between English settlements in New England and Virginia. Eventually, 13 separate colonies would be established along the East Coast.

The fact that American Indians were already living on this land was a mere technicality for Europeans such as Lord Baltimore. Native Americans were not Christians and therefore considered to be "godless" people. Without a Christian king, Indians could not own land, according to English laws. Half a century before the creation of the Maryland Colony, the famous Virginia explorer Sir Walter Raleigh had said the English had the right to occupy "such remote, heathen and barbarous lands, countries, and territories."

Indians did not own the land like "civilized" people, English colonists also believed, because they moved from place to place with the seasons. They did not

Thousands of American Indians lived in the area when the Maryland colonists arrived.

settle down in one place and build permanent homes, businesses, and cities. They did not draw and publish scientific maps, keep detailed written property records, or pay taxes to the king.

American Indians looked at land differently. Land and the resources it provided were something to be shared or borrowed and returned. They defined land in terms of its natural boundaries—its rivers, coastline, and mountains. They knew exactly what plants and animals lived within specific regions, and which tribes dominated each area. The Indians did not think of their land in terms of laws, like the English. The Earth, for them, had religious power. It was a living thing, like animals and plants—something to be used wisely, shared, and worshipped, but not owned.

Settlers like those sent by Lord Baltimore did not consider the possibility that Indians had their own equally rich culture, one that had evolved over thousands of years in North America. To British eyes, Maryland was still unoccupied land—wild, uncultivated, and ripe for picking.

When Lord Baltimore's party of about 140 people arrived in Maryland in 1634, thousands of Indians lived in the territory. However, the territory was his land now, a gift to his family given directly from the king. Lord Baltimore held the Charter of Maryland marked by the king's Great Seal of England. To keep all this real estate, Cecil believed, all he had to

Leonard Calvert established the colonial government in Maryland.

do was fill the land with settlers, build towns, and defend his territory from anyone—English, Spanish, or Indian—who tried to take it away.

For Lord Baltimore, land was power. It was proof of his nobility and something he could pass on to future members of the Calvert family. He was himself like the king of a small country. The more land he could control, the more powerful he could be. By renting the land to others, he could turn his land into wealth. By rewarding land to others—much like the king had rewarded land to him and to his father—he could build up his colony.

Lord Baltimore planned to quickly fill Maryland with people by trading land for work. That way, he did not have to spend his entire fortune building his colony. He promised 2,000 acres (800 hectares) to any man who agreed to bring along five servants.

The first 17 men who took the offer were mostly the sons of wealthy Catholic landowners. They paid the expenses for their indentured servants, who signed a contract to repay their debt with a few years' labor at the master's manor farm. When the contract was honored, these indentured servants could be free to own their own land.

Although it seems un-American today, colonists fully accepted the English idea that some people were born "better" than others. They accepted a system where a smaller and supposedly wiser group ruled over the working classes. The privileged gentry behaved in a refined way, dressed in fine clothes, and participated in the arts. A lord was expected to be wealthy, well dressed, and highly educated. He owned land and did not work with his hands, but with his mind.

To settlers who brought fewer than five servants, Lord Baltimore agreed to give 1,000 acres (400 hectares), plus 100 acres (40 hectares) per servant. Wives were valued at another 100 acres (40 hectares). Children over 16 and unmarried women were worth

50 acres (20 hectares) each.

Each landowner could keep his property for life, as long as he paid Lord Baltimore an annual fee called a quitrent for using the land. Each landowner had the power to make local laws, run the local court, and enforce his own rules on his manor farm. He also could pass on his property to his son, but if the landowner

The settlement of St. Mary's as it looked in its early years

had no heirs, or if he died without writing a will, his land and property returned to Lord Baltimore.

This system of land ownership was called a palatinate. In this system, one landlord managed a huge piece of territory—collecting rents year after year and never selling the land. When the landlord died, the rents were paid to his son. When people built homes in a palatinate, the landlord still collected rent on the land under the house. (This system of "ground rents" is still evident in the laws of Baltimore, Maryland, today.)

Although Lord Baltimore may have handled himself much like a king, he was in reality more like a prince. England's king still had the power to take the land charter away. To show that he was really in charge, King Charles required Lord Baltimore to present him with a token of his loyalty. So every year on Easter weekend, Lord Baltimore delivered two Indian arrows to the king.

While he was creating a colony from afar, Lord Baltimore was starting a family in England. His wife, Anne Arundell, gave birth to the couple's first child in 1634. The boy, named George, would never follow in his father's footsteps, though. George died in 1636. The next year, the couple's second son, Charles, was born. The Calverts went on to have three daughters, Anne, Mary, and Elizabeth. ☙

5 LIFE AMONG THE INDIANS

❧⟨✿⟩❧

In Maryland, Lord Baltimore's first colonists were nervous. In March 1634, the forests and isolated lands of America were almost as frightening as the unpredictable sea. At Point Comfort, Virginia, settlers had been warned that Indians in the area were readying for war. Twelve years earlier, the Powhatan Indians had killed 300 Virginians in a series of raids. Marylanders feared the same fate.

Many American Indians lived in the Chesapeake area. In the winter, they wore long cloaks, leggings, and moccasins. Some painted the upper half of their faces blue, decorated themselves in colorful feathers, and tied their long, dark hair to the side with strings of connected shells. In warmer temperatures, they would be painted in red oil to

Leonard Calvert and the Maryland colonists agreed to live alongside Indians in a settlement that became the colony's capital.

A replica of the Dove *docked at the harbor of St. Mary's*

ward off biting insects. The English visitors were horrified at first by such unfamiliar sights. At night, the foreign travelers nervously watched the Indian fires that flickered through the trees.

Unsure what to expect from the Indians or where to settle, most of the colonists stayed with the *Ark* at St. Clement's Island. Following Lord Baltimore's instructions to make friends with natives, Leonard Calvert and a small group of men continued upriver in the *Dove*. While in Virginia, Leonard had hired a guide named Henry Fleet. He was an English fur trader who had spent a decade among the coastal Indians from the Chesapeake to Canada, and spoke native languages fluently. On the *Dove*, they traveled first up the Potomac River to meet with the emperor of the Piscataway Indians, then went south, past St. Clements Island, to a river only 10 miles (16 km) from Chesapeake Bay. Fleet directed them to the village of the Yaocomaco Indians on the western bank of the St. George River. This turned out to be the best possible advice.

The Yaocomaco made an appealing offer to the white settlers. They agreed to share their village and live together in harmony with the newcomers. They divided their village in half, giving one side to the settlers. In exchange, the Indians received English-made cloth, hoes, and axes—along with a promise the settlers would protect their hosts against raids by rival tribes. On March 27, 1634, after a journey of nearly four months, the travelers finally came ashore for good. They renamed the village St. Mary's. Following

Captain Henry Fleet was a rough-and-tumble businessman, who traveled along the East Coast and up rivers to trade with inland people. He saw Indians as business partners, and they supplied him with thousands of beaver pelts that he sold in England. He also traded with early colonists in Virginia, Massachusetts, Canada, and the Isles of Shoals in New Hampshire. After being held prisoner by one Indian tribe for five years, he claimed he nearly forgot how to speak English.

Like tribes in nearby Virginia, the Yaocomaco lived in longhouses that they called witchotts. Each longhouse was made from two rows of saplings bent together at the top and fastened. The long curved hut was then covered in sheets of bark or woven mats made of reeds. A smoky central fire vented through a hole in the ceiling. Some witchotts were designed to let in air and light by rolling up some mats.

Lord Baltimore's instructions, they immediately began building fortifications, a storehouse, a guardhouse, and a church.

For a brief time, Maryland seemed like heaven on Earth. Father White's notes sounded like a description of the biblical Garden of Eden. "I have never seen a greater and more delightful river," White wrote to Lord Baltimore. The fertile soil, he said, produced food all by itself. The dense woods were carpeted with wild strawberries. There were fresh nuts, fruit trees, sassafras, and grapevines. Natural springs flowed with pure water. There was plenty of game for meat and an endless variety of colorful birds, including eagles, swans, ducks, geese, and herons.

The close bond between the whites and Indians helped Lord Baltimore's colony get a strong start during the critical first year. Almost all the first arrivals were men, and they moved into Indian homes and took over existing gardens. Their lives were quite comfortable, according to White. Indian women and children helped with household and planting chores for the settlers, while the Indian men

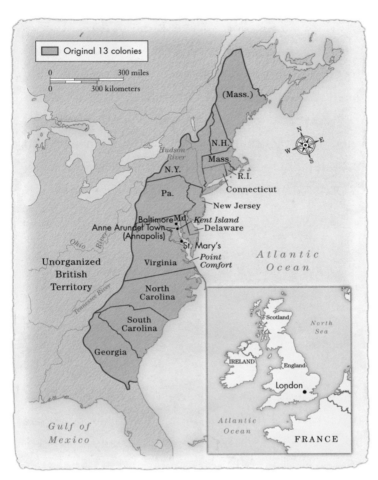

The Maryland Colony began with St. Mary's and grew along Chesapeake Bay.

brought in fresh meat. They provided deer, turkeys, squirrels, and fish, either as gifts or in trade. Thanks to Lord Baltimore's careful planning, the colony included not only carpenters and builders, but experienced farmers who brought along lots of seeds. Tutored by the Indians and benefiting from rich soil, the St. Mary's settlers enjoyed an excellent first harvest.

Although he did not speak the native language and relied on translators, Father White worked to convert the natives to the Catholic religion. He quickly came to admire and respect the Yaocomaco as he lived among them day to day. He described them in his journal as polite, attractive, intelligent, rational, noble, and cheerful. White was especially impressed by their hunting abilities. He wrote:

> *They shoot these arrows with such great skill that they pierce a sparrow through the middle from a distance, and in order to practice [this] skill they throw a thong of leather into the air, then they release an arrow from the bowstring and pierce the thong before it falls down.*

The Indians were clearly religious, and White reported on a tribal ceremony held around a huge bonfire. Indians came from great distances, passed around a ceremonial pipe, and offered prayers to a higher power. He noted that the people told stories of an ancient flood that once covered the world, similar to the biblical tale of Noah's Ark.

The experiment in tolerance was working. Catholics, Protestants, and Native Americans functioned like a team. Maryland appeared to have a spirit of compromise not evident in New England to the north or Virginia to the south. It was a comfortable

"middle temperature," according to White, that "enjoys the advantages, and escapes the evils, of each." Lord Baltimore was so pleased on reading White's report that he immediately had it published in England.

In a letter to Lord Baltimore, Leonard reported:

> *Our success, dear brother, is due to your vision and planning, to our father's costly experience at Newfoundland and to the generous help of the Maryland Indians.*

Back in England, Lord Baltimore received tokens of the success of his colony—some Maryland-grown Indian corn, beaver pelts, a wampum necklace for Lady Anne, a few arrows, and a beautiful native basket woven from grass. ℘

6 TROUBLE IN PARADISE

⤔⟨×⟩⤝

In 1635, the sense of peaceful cooperation left the settlement called St. Mary's. The Yaocomaco quietly withdrew from the village, and Lord Baltimore's colonists feared the Indians were preparing a surprise attack. But in reality, the trouble was started by other English settlers.

According to Leonard Calvert and Father White, Protestants in Virginia had been spreading false rumors about the Catholic newcomers. They told the Yaocomaco that the Marylanders were actually Spanish conquerors who had come to steal all the Indians' land. Once Leonard was able to communicate with the Yaocomaco, he explained the situation and persuaded them to return home. Still, the calm of the Maryland Colony had been broken.

Tensions between Maryland and Virginia colonists erupted into a battle on Chesapeake Bay.

Born the year after his brother Cecil, Leonard Calvert (1606–1647) gets much credit for making the Maryland Colony work. As the colony's first governor, he had control of daily affairs, while his brother sent orders from England. Leonard had the difficult task of balancing Lord Baltimore's master plan with the strong views of the Maryland Assembly. Leonard found time to return to England twice for meetings with his older brother. During those visits, Leonard married and fathered two children who later immigrated to Maryland.

Lord Baltimore had long been wary of the Virginians, particularly William Claiborne, the Kent Island fur trader who had earlier challenged the Calverts' charter for Maryland and who may have spread the rumors to the Yaocomaco. Although King Charles had sided with the Calverts in that dispute, he remained sympathetic to Claiborne and other Virginia Protestants living on land granted to Lord Baltimore. The king thought that they should be left alone. Lord Baltimore, however, insisted that he owned the land and the right to protect it from enemies like Claiborne. From England, Lord Baltimore sent orders to his colonists to arrest Claiborne and seize his property if he did not abide by the Maryland charter.

The resulting feud led to one of the first naval battles in American history. Following orders from Lord Baltimore, a Maryland commissioner named Thomas Cornwallis seized a small boat owned by Claiborne. In retaliation, Claiborne armed another pinnace and sent 14 men to reclaim his boat. In early spring of 1635, Claiborne's ship faced off against two small Maryland ships on the Pocomoke River. The cannon battle lasted only a few minutes. Four men died—three on Claiborne's side, including his ship's captain. Claiborne had lost, but the battle was far from over. In fact, the dispute was so tense that when the governor of Virginia failed to condemn Maryland's attack on Kent Island, he was arrested by his own citizens and shipped back to England.

Lord Baltimore, who still had plans to travel to Maryland, had an idea he thought might solve the border problem. He quietly suggested the king make him the governor of Virginia, which would let him oversee both colonies. But the king did not think that putting a Catholic lord in charge of a Protestant colony was a good idea. After the setback, Lord Baltimore remained in England and oversaw his colony from afar.

His next struggle was with his own colony. Now in his early 30s, Lord Baltimore imagined himself as the undisputed leader of Maryland. Still, he had agreed to listen to the Assembly of Marylanders, a council run by his brother and key landowners in the colony. In 1638, the Assembly decided it would not accept his total authority to create laws from far away in England. The settlers wanted to govern themselves. At first, Lord Baltimore fought back by shutting down the Maryland government for nearly a year, but he eventually compromised. The settlers could write their own laws governing the colony, Lord Baltimore agreed, but he held on to his right to veto any laws he disliked. It would be a power he rarely used, so the Marylanders largely did run their own affairs from then on.

The good news in Lord Baltimore's colony was the immediate success of tobacco farming, which caused the colony to grow quickly. Choice plots of land along Chesapeake Bay had been divided among the early settlers and blossomed into large manor farms and smaller tobacco plantations. The promise of fertile land and quick profits attracted more settlers. Others were drawn there because the colony welcomed both Protestants and Catholics, along with indentured servants and slaves from Africa and the Caribbean who were eventually brought to work the expanding farms. Settlers and their workers cut down the ancient forests to make way for tobacco fields. The large, leafy plants were so central to life in Maryland that tobacco could be used in place of money.

More cultivated land in Maryland meant more rental income for Lord Baltimore, and he needed money badly. His investment in settling his colony had tapped most of the wealth he had inherited from his father, making him almost entirely dependent on his aging father-in-law, Lord Arundell, for funds and a place to live.

While Maryland was thriving, England was coming apart. The Puritans, a religious group opposed to the king and his Church of England, were growing very powerful. Slowly, they had gained more and more control in the English Parliament. The Puritans rallied behind a man named Oliver Cromwell, who was popular with many of the English. King Charles and his supporters were in trouble. This battle for control of the English government spilled over into the American colonies.

In February 1645, the merchant ship *Reformation* sailed into the harbor at St. Mary's. The captain of the

King Charles faced unrest in England that eventually cost him his throne and his life.

ship was a man named Richard Ingle. He had been to Maryland before to trade with the colonists. Two years earlier, he had been arrested and jailed in St. Mary's when he spoke out against King Charles, whom the Marylanders liked and supported. This time, Ingle came to seize control of the Catholic settlement and get his revenge. He came with armed men and written permission from the English Parliament to plunder the town.

In what became known as Ingle's Rebellion, he and his men took over the best houses in the region, looted their contents, and tossed out Maryland's governing Assembly. They burned other homes and killed livestock. They ransacked the Catholic church—the only one of its kind in the colonies—and shipped Father White back to England in chains. Claiborne, reportedly working in cooperation with Ingle, took back his trading post at Kent Island.

There is no record of Lord Baltimore's actions or whereabouts during this time. As a friend of the king under a Puritan rebellion, he was unable to take action to protect Maryland. If he was living in London, he kept a low profile. He likely considered his Maryland to be lost forever.

However, his brother fought to regain the family's colony. After being driven out, Leonard managed to build up a small militia in Virginia by offering to pay volunteers a healthy reward. This group returned to

St. Mary's and ended Ingle's Rebellion in late 1646.

Lord Baltimore's colony survived, thanks to his brother, but it was traumatized. The golden days were over. The population, once as high as 600, was not much larger now than when the *Ark* and *Dove* had dropped off the first settlers.

Worse yet, soon after retaking St. Mary's, Leonard died at age 41 after a sudden and mysterious illness.

Leonard Calvert became ill soon after regaining control of Maryland on behalf of Lord Baltimore.

> *"Take all and pay all,"*
> *Leonard Calvert had*
> *told Margaret Brent,*
> *and that is exactly*
> *what she did. To settle*
> *Maryland's debts,*
> *Brent had to sell some*
> *of Lord Baltimore's*
> *goods, an action that*
> *angered him. He*
> *accused her of "med-*
> *dling" with his private*
> *property, but the leaders*
> *of Maryland followed*
> *her orders. Later, how-*
> *ever, when she peti-*
> *tioned the Maryland*
> *Assembly to allow her*
> *to vote, the men turned*
> *her down.*

One account suggests that he died from the bite of a poisonous snake. Leonard died so soon after putting an end to the rebellion that he left the army of Virginian soldiers who had defeated Ingle unpaid. This created a potentially dangerous situation for the weakened colony that now had no governor.

In his last days, however, Leonard had made a wise decision. In front of important members of the Assembly, he appointed a woman named Margaret Brent to take care of his property and act on his behalf. Brent was unmarried and may have been related to the Calverts in some way. Still, it was very rare in the 1600s for a woman to be given so much power. But Mistress Brent, as she was known, was respected in the colony, and Leonard trusted she would do the right thing. Brent sold off many of Leonard's possessions and property to pay the soldiers.

Despite his grief over the death of his brother, Lord Baltimore also made a wise move. He appointed a Protestant named William Stone to be the next governor of Maryland. This move offended

neither the king's supporters nor the Puritans, and calmed those who feared the Calverts were building a Catholic colony in the New World. ✑

Margaret Brent took on a leadership role that was unusual for a woman of her era.

Chapter

7 TOLERANCE AND TURMOIL

❦

In 1649, Lord Baltimore made history. His strong steps to make Maryland a welcoming place for all Christians—no matter what religious practices they followed—would become his greatest legacy, the thing for which he is most remembered. He urged the members of the Assembly to pass the Act Concerning Religion, often called the Act of Toleration. This law required that Protestants and Catholics treat each other with respect, even forbidding them to call each other names.

The law was groundbreaking; however, it provided limited tolerance compared to what Americans enjoy today. Then, the protection of religious freedom applied only to members of the Christian faith. People practicing other faiths could

A copy of Lord Baltimore's Act of Toleration

A LAW
OF
MARYLAND
Concerning
RELIGION.

Oraſmuch as is a well-governed and Chriſtian Commonwealth, Matters concerning Religion and the Honour of God ought to be in the firſt place to be taken into ſerious conſideration, and endeavoured to be ſettled. Be it therefore Ordained and Enacted by the Right Honourable *CÆCILIUS* Lord Baron of *Baltemore*, abſolute Lord and Proprietary of this Province, with the Advice and Conſent of the Upper and Lower Houſe of this General Aſſembly, That whatſoever perſon or perſons within this Province and the Iſlands thereunto belonging, ſhall from henceforth blaſpheme G O D, that is curſe him; or ſhall deny our Saviour J E S U S C H R I S T to be the Son of God; or ſhall deny the Holy Trinity, the Father, Son, & Holy Ghoſt; or the Godhead of any of the ſaid Three Perſons of the Trinity, or the Unity of the Godhead, or ſhall uſe or utter any reproachful ſpeeches, words, or language, concerning the Holy Trinity, or any of the ſaid three Perſons thereof, ſhall be puniſhed with death, and confiſcation or forfeiture of all his or her Lands and Goods to the Lord Proprietary and his Heirs.

And be it alſo enacted by the Authority, and with the advice and aſſent aforeſaid, That whatſoever perſon or perſons ſhall from henceforth uſe or utter any reproachful words or ſpeeches concerning the bleſſed Virgin *MARY*, the Mother of our Saviour, or the holy Apoſtles or Evangeliſts, or any of them, ſhall in ſuch caſe for the firſt Offence forfeit to the ſaid Lord Proprietary and his Heirs, Lords and Proprietaries of this Province, the ſum of Five pounds Sterling, or the value thereof to be levied on the goods and chattels of every ſuch perſon ſo offending; but in caſe ſuch offender or offenders ſhall not then have goods and chattels ſufficient for the ſatisfying of ſuch forfeiture, or that the ſame be not otherwiſe ſpeedily ſatisfied, that then ſuch offender or offenders ſhall be publickly whipt, and be impriſoned during the pleaſure of the Lord Proprietary, or the Lieutenant or Chief Governor of this Province for the time being; And that every ſuch offender and offenders for every ſecond offence ſhall forfeit Ten Pounds Sterling, or the value thereof to be levied as aforeſaid; or in caſe ſuch offender or offenders ſhall not then have goods and chattels within this Province ſufficient for that purpoſe, then to be publickly and ſeverely whipt and impriſoned as before is expreſſed; and that every perſon or perſons before mentioned, offending herein the third time, ſhall for ſuch third offence, forfeit all his lands and goods, and be for ever baniſht and expelled out of this Province.

And be it alſo further Enacted by the ſame Authority, advice, and aſſent, That whatſoever perſon or perſons ſhall from henceforth upon any occaſion of offence, or otherwiſe in a reproachful manner or way, declare, call, or denominate, any perſon or perſons whatſoever, inhabiting, reſiding, trafficking, trading, or commercing within this Province, or within any the Ports, Harbors, Creeks or Havens to the ſame belonging, an Heretick, Schiſmatick, Idolater, Puritan, Preſbyterian, Independant, Popiſh Prieſt, Jeſuit, Jeſuited Papiſt, Lutheran, Calviniſt, Anabaptiſt, Browniſt, Antinomian, Roundhead, Separatiſt, or other name or term in a reproachfull manner relating to matter of Religion, ſhall for every ſuch offence forfeit and loſe the ſum of Ten ſhillings Sterling, or the value thereof, to be levied of the goods and chattels of every ſuch offender and offenders, the one half thereof to be forfeited and paid unto the perſon ſo offended, of whom ſuch reproachfull words are, or ſhall be ſpoken or uttered, and the other half thereof to the Lord Proprietary and his Heirs, Lords and Proprietaries of this Province: But if ſuch perſon or perſons who ſhall at any time utter or ſpeak any ſuch reproachfull words or language, ſhall not have goods or chattels ſufficient and overt within this Province to be taken to ſatiſfy the penalty aforeſaid, or that the ſame be not otherwiſe ſpeedily ſatiſfied, that then the perſon and perſons ſo offending ſhall be publickly whipt, and ſhall ſuffer impriſonment without Bail or Mainpriſe untill he, ſhe, or they, reſpectively, ſhall ſatisfie the party ſo offended or grieved for ſuch reproachfull Language, by asking him or her reſpectively forgiveneſs publickly, for ſuch his offence, before the Magiſtrate or chief Officer or Officers of the Town or place where ſuch offence ſhall be given.

And be further likewiſe enacted by the authority and conſent aforeſaid, that every perſon and perſons within this Province, that ſhall at any time hereafter prophane the Sabbath, or Lords day, called Sunday, by frequent ſwearing, drunkenneſs, or by any uncivil or diſorderly Recreation, or by working on that day when abſolute neceſſity doth not require, ſhall for every ſuch firſt offence forfeit two ſhillings ſix pence Sterling, or the value thereof; and for the ſecond offence five ſhillings Sterling, or the value thereof; and for every time he ſhall offend in like manner afterwards, Ten ſhillings Sterling, or the value thereof; and in caſe ſuch offender or offenders ſhall not have ſufficient goods or chattels within this Province to ſatisfy any of the aforeſaid penalties reſpectively hereby impoſed for prophaning the Sabbath or Lords day called Sunday as aforeſaid, then in every ſuch caſe the party ſo offending ſhall for the firſt and ſecond offence in that kind be impriſoned till he or ſhe ſhall publickly in open Court before the chief Commander, Judge or Magiſtrate of that County, Town, or Precinct wherein ſuch offence ſhall be committed, acknowledge the ſcandal and offence he hath in that reſpect given, againſt God, and the good and civil Government of this Province: and for the third offence and for every time after ſhall alſo be publickly whipt.

And whereas the inforcing of the Conſcience in matter of Religion hath frequently fallen out to be of dangerous conſequence in thoſe Commonwealths where it hath been practiſed, and for the more quiet and peaceable Government of this Province, and the better to preſerve mutual love & unity amongſt the Inhabitants here, Be it therefore alſo by the Lord Proprietary with the advice and aſſent of this Aſſembly, ordained and enacted, except as in this preſent Act is before declared and ſet forth, that no perſon or perſons whatſoever within this Province, or the Iſlands, Ports, Harbors, Creeks, or Havens thereunto belonging, profeſſing to believe in Jeſus Chriſt, ſhall from henceforth be any ways troubled, moleſted, or diſcountenanced, for, or in reſpect of his or her Religion nor in the free exerciſe thereof within this Province or the Iſlands thereunto belonging, nor any way compelled to the belief or exerciſe of any other Religion againſt his or her conſent, ſo as they be not unfaithfull to the Lord Proprietary, or moleſt or conſpire againſt the civil Government, eſtabliſhed or to be eſtabliſhed in this Province under him and his Heirs. And that all and every perſon and perſons that ſhall preſume contrary to this Act and the true intent & meaning thereof, directly or indirectly, either in perſon or eſtate, wilfully to wrong, diſturb, or trouble, or moleſt any perſon or perſons whatſoever within this Province, profeſſing to believe in Jeſus Chriſt, for or in reſpect of his or her Religion, or the free exerciſe thereof within this Province, otherwiſe then is provided for in this Act, that ſuch perſon or perſons ſo offending ſhall be compelled to pay treble damages to the party ſo wronged or moleſted, and for every ſuch offence ſhall alſo forfeit Twenty ſhillings Sterling in Money, or the value thereof, half thereof for the uſe of the Lord Proprietary and his Heirs, Lords and Proprietaries of this Province, and the other half thereof for the uſe of the Party ſo wronged or moleſted as aforeſaid; or if the party ſo offending as aforeſaid, ſhall refuſe or be unable to recompence the party ſo wronged, or to ſatisfy ſuch fine or forfeiture, then ſuch offender ſhall be ſeverely puniſhed by publick whipping and impriſonment during the pleaſure of the Lord Proprietary or his Lieutenant or chief Governor of this Province for the time being, without Bail or Mainpriſe.

And be it further alſo enacted by the authority and conſent aforeſaid, that the Sheriff or other Officer or Officers from time to time to be appointed and authorized for that purpoſe of the County, Town, or Precinct where any ſuch offence in this preſent Act contained, ſhall happen at any time to be committed, and whereupon there is hereby a forfeiture, fine, or penalty impoſed, ſhall from time to time diſtrain and ſeize the goods and eſtate of every ſuch perſon ſo offending as aforeſaid againſt this preſent Act or any part thereof, and ſell the ſame or any part thereof for the full ſatisfaction of ſuch forfeiture, fine, or penalty as aforeſaid, reſtoring to the party ſo offending, the remainder or over-plus of the ſaid goods or eſtate, after ſuch ſatisfaction ſo made as aforeſaid.

still, on rare occasions, be punished with death. But for its time, the Act of Toleration was revolutionary.

The law was also smart business for Lord Baltimore. Richard Ingle's year of plundering had driven many colonists out of Maryland, and Lord Baltimore needed to attract all sorts of people. Many settlers from other colonies soon began moving to Maryland in search of land, work, and religious freedom. As many as 300 Puritans left nearby Virginia the same year and settled the town of Providence in Maryland.

Back in England, family problems were taking a toll on Lord Baltimore. His father-in-law, who had provided financial support during lean times, had died in 1648. The next year, Lord Baltimore's wife, Anne, died unexpectedly at the age of 34. He would never marry again.

The spirit of tolerance Lord Baltimore encouraged in Maryland was nowhere to be found in England. Radical Protestants under Oliver Cromwell had taken over the English government. Cromwell had argued against the Church of England, the country's official religion. King Charles preferred to worship in a manner that was filled with rituals that Puritans such as Cromwell considered too similar to the Catholic practices that they violently opposed. With Cromwell in control, King Charles was jailed and beheaded.

The overthrow of the king was a blow to Lord Baltimore. King Charles had granted him the Maryland charter, and the colony was named after the queen. With the king gone, everything Lord Baltimore owned was at risk. He considered fleeing from England to live in Maryland, but once again he chose to stay and face the trouble.

Lord Baltimore might have lost his title, his colony, or even his life after the execution of King

Charles. He was, after all, both a supporter of the king and a Catholic, whom the Puritans bitterly opposed. But like his father, Lord Baltimore understood how to move with political winds. He had already appointed a Protestant governor in Maryland after Leonard's death—a move that comforted his opponents—and now he rode out the political storm.

Two of Lord Baltimore's old foes challenged his control of Maryland once again. William Claiborne, who was now the leader of Virginia's government, and Richard Ingle suggested that Cromwell take the Maryland charter away from the Calvert family. They urged Cromwell to merge Maryland and Virginia into one colony. Lord Baltimore responded with a written report delivered to the Protestant government. He offered clear reasons why Maryland should remain an independent colony under his control. It had remained loyal to the English government, and, in fact, Maryland had recently welcomed Puritans forced from the less-tolerant Virginia Colony. Lord Baltimore's arguments swayed Cromwell.

In 1653, Cromwell dissolved the entire British Parliament and declared himself to be the lone Protector of England. He was now even more powerful than a king. Again, Lord Baltimore did what was necessary to protect his interests in America. He convinced Cromwell to give him control of Maryland, whose governor asked colonists to swear

a loyalty oath to the new Protector of England. Without leaving England, Lord Baltimore took care of Maryland, a successful colony where tobacco growing continued to be a profitable business.

Oliver Cromwell threw out Parliament and took sole power over England's government.

In Virginia, Claiborne grew frustrated, and he became a key person behind a move to get rid of Maryland's Governor Stone. Claiborne and Virginia's governor threw Stone out and replaced him with a Puritan. A new Assembly was installed in Maryland, and the spirit of tolerance in the colony fell apart. The all-Protestant leadership changed the Act of Toleration so that it no longer protected those who did not follow the Puritan religion.

Lord Baltimore again took action in England. He pleaded his case to Cromwell, and he sent a letter to Stone ordering the former governor to raise an army quickly and fight to win Maryland back, just like Leonard Calvert had done a decade before. On March 24, 1655, Stone's militia of 135 men met a slightly larger force at the Puritan town of Providence, Maryland. It would not be a good day for his militia, however. Stone's forces attacked by land and by sea, but the larger Puritan militia, aided by two ships in the harbor, crushed the attack.

Historical re-enactors prepare to recreate the 1655 battle for control of the Maryland Colony.

Claiborne and the Puritans won the battle, but they had gone too far. Cromwell was annoyed with

the Puritan takeover in Maryland and the brutal defeat of Lord Baltimore's men. Even after winning Maryland, the Puritans continued to complain to Cromwell about the Catholics. Meanwhile, they took over St. Mary's, the colony's capital, and trashed the official records of the colony. Cromwell decided that Lord Baltimore, despite being a Catholic, looked like a better leader, and two years after the battle at Providence, he turned the colony of Maryland back over to Lord Baltimore.

Now in control, Lord Baltimore quickly appointed a new governor and modernized the government. He increased the size of the militia by drafting Maryland men into service. To clear up border disputes, he ordered a survey of the entire colony and published a detailed map. With the Act of Toleration back to its original form, Maryland welcomed a fresh wave of French, Swedish, German, and Dutch immigrants.

In September 1658, Oliver Cromwell died. The following year, England welcomed Charles II as king. Lord Baltimore and his colony had survived the unrest in England, much like his colonists aboard the *Ark* and *Dove* had survived terrible weather and brutal seas 25 years earlier. ❧

8 PROFITS AND HUMAN COSTS

❧⌘❧

George Calvert had pinned his fortune on fish, until the frigid Canadian winter drove him southward. His son, the second Lord Baltimore, would make a fortune from a leafy plant. The success of Maryland and other American colonies was closely tied to the rise of tobacco sales. Virginians began selling the dried leaves in 1614, two decades before Lord Baltimore's colonists settled in nearby Maryland. By then, pipe smoking had become popular in England and much of Europe.

Early Spanish traders had started the industry when they discovered natives in the West Indies using tobacco. Two Virginians—Sir Walter Raleigh in the 1580s and later John Rolfe in the 1620s—are best known for promoting tobacco in England. Raleigh

Slave labor fueled the economic growth of Maryland and other American colonies.

made it fashionable, and Rolfe, who married the
Indian woman Pocahontas, made growing tobacco
profitable in the Chesapeake Bay region. Growers
and users of tobacco at the time did not know it was
addictive and could cause cancer. In fact, tobacco

*Sir Walter
Raleigh on board
his ship*

was promoted as a healthy cure for many ailments. But not everyone supported tobacco use.

King James I, for whom George Calvert worked devotedly, had once called smoking a disgusting habit. In 1604, he wrote, "Smoking is a custom loathsome to the eye, hateful to the nose, harmful to the brain, dangerous to the lungs." He originally tried to tax the product out of existence. But the public became so attracted to pipe smoking that the king reversed his view and encouraged the lucrative business.

Tobacco was the ideal crop for Lord Baltimore's colony. Tobacco required a great deal of open land to grow, and it thrived along the rivers of the Chesapeake region. Lord Baltimore collected rent from the owners of large manor farms, who were free to run their plantations with little interference from the colonial government. The rents they paid allowed Lord Baltimore to slowly build back his fortune.

Growing tobacco required lots of people to do

At the time of the founding of Maryland, tobacco was already the subject of controversy. Tobacco use was growing in countries as distant as Sweden and Korea, but smoking was banned in some countries, including Japan and Switzerland. The pope threatened to excommunicate Catholics who used snuff. In Russia, a first-time smoker could be whipped or have his nose split. While the French relaxed regulations on tobacco in 1637, Chinese and Turkish laws said smokers could be punished with death.

Farm workers harvest tobacco leaves on a Chesapeake Bay region farm.

the planting, raising, harvesting, drying, and curing. At first, Maryland's plantation owners got their labor from indentured servants. But those servants eventually worked off their obligation to the owner and then wanted to collect the land they were due and become farmers on their own. As plantations grew, more laborers were needed. In Virginia, more and more of that labor was coming from slaves, who were sometimes Indians but were mostly black people from the West Indies and Africa.

By studying Virginia and Maryland laws during Lord Baltimore's lifetime, historians have clearly traced the evol-- ution of slavery in America. At first, when most of the workers were indentured servants, colonial laws treated black and white servants equally. As more black slaves were brought to the area, laws changed. All slaves were servants, the early Maryland law said, but not all servants were enslaved.

Indentured servants gener- ally became servants voluntarily. Most signed a contract agreeing to work for an employer for a set period of time. Many "worked off" the cost of their trip to America by becoming servants to the person who paid their passage. At the end of the contracted time, the servants were considered free. Slaves, however, were servants with little hope of gaining freedom. Many had been kidnapped from their homelands and sold as if they were objects.

Because the value of tobacco kept chang- ing, Lord Baltimore decided to stabilize the economy by making his own money for use in Maryland. In the late 1650s, he had the coins designed and struck with his picture on them. In England, he was almost arrested for minting his own money, a power reserved for the king. But his charter, he proved, gave him the right to mint coins. Lord Baltimore's coins were used for at least 10 years, but the idea was not very successful. Today, the few coins that survive are very valuable to collectors.

Slavery was introduced in the colonies in 1619.

While indentured servants could be black or white, most slaves brought to Maryland were black people. The word *slave* first appeared in Maryland court records as early as 1638, and in time, any black person in Lord Baltimore's colony was assumed to be a slave.

As tobacco plantations grew larger, the rights of these workers shrank. By 1662, neither black slaves nor white servants were allowed to travel more than 2 miles (3.2 km) from their plantation without a written note from the owner. Slaves were not allowed to carry weapons. White servants who ran away from their homes in the company of black slaves were punished with added years as servants. White women who married enslaved men were forced to become servants, and their children became slaves.

In 1664, Maryland went further than any other American colony when it decreed that slaves were *durante vita*, or enslaved for life. Black slavery became fully accepted by Maryland law. The children of slaves inherited their father's slavery in the same way that Lord Baltimore had inherited his father's land. This law coincided with the drop in tobacco prices in the European market. By giving

In 1672, the British government would get into the business of buying and selling human beings. England created the Royal African Company, which later gave way to private slave importers. As Maryland grew, so did its enslaved population. Colonial records track the slaves' arrivals. For example, records show a ship arriving in Maryland with 160 slaves in 1695. The next year 175 people were delivered in bondage. In 1695, the governor reported 450 slaves brought into the colony. Maryland's tobacco economy was becoming fully dependent upon slaves.

Tobacco leaves were so valuable that they could be used like money.

slaves no possible path to freedom, Maryland farmers could ensure themselves access to a cheap, captive workforce, even during hard economic times. Plantation owners turned to slavery in a big way. Men, women, and children were taken from Africa against their will and transported under horrific conditions aboard ships to be bought and sold like property.

Early records show rare cases in which a "Negro" or "African" was able to win freedom, but discrimination based solely on skin color was already written deeply into the laws of Maryland. The result was that Maryland created a permanent and growing population of slaves. As workers, they had valuable skills, but they went largely unpaid. Plantations were located miles apart, isolating slaves and making escape difficult. In Lord Baltimore's Maryland and elsewhere, the American form of slavery was on the rise.

Yet Marylanders still considered their colony more tolerant than others. To show their tolerance, Marylanders allowed slaves to be baptized into the Christian faith, a practice not allowed in neighboring Virginia. From Lord Baltimore's viewpoint, he was providing slaves who became Christians a chance to save their souls and go to heaven.

However, the Maryland government passed another law stating that black slaves, even when they became Christians, remained enslaved. While their souls could be set free, their bodies could not. ✄

9 PASSING DOWN POWER

❧❧❧

Just as he had been tested as a young man, Lord Baltimore would test his only surviving son. Charles Calvert was just 23 in 1661 when his father named him governor of the Maryland Colony, thrusting leadership upon him at an early age. Charles and his wife, Mary, arrived at St. Mary's with great celebration. For the next half-century, Charles would struggle to develop his father's colony.

Charles was no ordinary pioneer. He was the son of a wealthy and powerful English baron. His father and grandfather had been friendly with kings. He had been raised in luxury and privilege. Charles arrived in Maryland with 30 servants and slaves to attend to his every need. He lived in a mansion with the finest furnishings. He threw the biggest parties in town.

Lord Baltimore's son Charles became Maryland's governor and lived with his family in St. Mary's.

Philip Calvert was only 6 years old when his father, George Calvert, died. He was raised by his half-brother, Lord Baltimore, and his wife. After sending Philip to school in Portugal, Lord Baltimore made him his secretary in England, assisting in managing the colony. Lord Baltimore appointed Philip as a temporary governor of Maryland after a failed revolt. Philip's lead coffin was recently discovered in St. Mary's City. Scientists who examined the remains discovered that Philip was overweight, suffered from arthritis, stood 5-foot-6 (168 centimeters), and may have had reddish hair.

Charles also scrapped with his Uncle Philip, who had served as governor before he arrived in the Maryland Colony. Lord Baltimore had been satisfied with the job his younger brother had done as governor, but he felt obliged to turn the colony over to his oldest son. Charles took orders only from his father—to whom he wrote regularly.

When his wife died, Charles married a wealthy Maryland widow named Jane Sewall. He expected that their son, named Cecil in honor of the baby's grandfather, would someday inherit all of Maryland. Charles was so proud that he took his son, who was nicknamed Cis, all the way to England to meet his grandfather. Lord Baltimore and his grandson posed together for a portrait, with the younger Cecil holding a map of the Maryland Colony. (Unfortunately, the boy would die early in his teenage years.)

In England, Lord Baltimore looked forward to every bit of communication from Charles, but the

This Northerne part of Virginia (the limitts whereof extend farther Southwards) is heere inserted for the better description of the entrance into the Bay of Chesapeack.

NouaTERRÆ—MARIÆ, tabula

VIRGINIÆ PARS

CHE SA PE ACK bay

RS

OCEANVS ORIENTALIS.

Sea Leagues

James towne

Charles Ct.

Anne-Arundell

Dorchester Ct. Talbot Ct.

Sommerset Ct.

Nouæ Iersy Pars

ANGLIÆ PARS

A 1670s map of the Maryland Colony, the Chesapeake Bay, and the Potomac River, with locations labeled in Latin

few surviving letters do not shed much light on their relationship. Charles' letters to his father focused largely on politics, crops, taxes, land, and money. In one letter, Charles mentioned that he was sending some dried peaches from his wife, two wildcat pelts, and some black walnut wood for a shuffleboard table. Charles said he was thinking of building a brick house for Cis. He thanked his father for sending "a little boy," most likely a slave, to serve Cis. But the boy, Charles explained, was "a greate Theife" and could not remain with the governor's family. Then Charles mentioned another gift: "I have also Received ... my mothers picture which will be a great Ornament to my Parlor ... though the Painter hath not done it for her advantage."

Charles would prove to be a competent leader, but without the vision, patience, and political skills of his father. When Charles was disappointed or angry, he did not hide his feelings toward some of Maryland's people. He easily grew impatient with the problems of the lower classes. What did he care if one man's pig stole another man's corn? Why should he worry about broken window panes or bounties paid on wolf hides? Charles believed he had more serious issues to deal with, including a great hurricane that toppled houses and ruined tobacco crops in 1667— the same year St. Mary's was incorporated as St. Mary's City. Also, the king now wanted his colonies to sell tobacco only to England, which angered many colonists. There were problems everywhere.

Yet Charles did many good things for Maryland on Lord Baltimore's behalf. He improved the roads, built new courthouses and jails, and established four new counties. He also improved the structure of the government and made it possible for many landowners, mostly Catholics, to expand their fortunes.

Lord Baltimore remained far away in England, isolated from the troubles of his colony. He had lived to an old age for a man of his era, and he had seen the Maryland Colony through decades of struggle and growth. On November 30, 1675, Cecil Calvert died at home in Middlesex, England. The second Lord Baltimore was laid to rest after a quiet ceremony in a London church. He was 70 years old at the time of his death.

In Maryland, the man who had nurtured the colony seemed to simply disappear. The early records of the colony include no report of his death, and they note no reaction or tribute by the residents. He was a man they had never met or even seen, except as an image on a printed page or on the coins he had minted in the late 1650s. He was unknown in his own colony, except by his letters, his guiding hand, and the presence of his son, Charles, who would become the third Lord Baltimore. ✌

Lord Baltimore died in 1675, but his life had a lasting influence in Maryland.

10 A LASTING IMPACT

సొంసారు

In 1676, the year following Cecil Calvert's death, Marylanders completed one of the most important buildings in St. Mary's City, a new brick statehouse that stood at one end of town. A beautiful church, built in 1677, would soon stand at the other end. The buildings served as proof of the success of Cecil Calvert and his belief that the church and the government should be run separately. But the powerful influence of the colony's founder soon began to fade.

For most of the next century, control of Maryland would pass from one of Cecil's descendants to the next. A total of six men would hold the title of Lord Baltimore, but none of those who followed could match Cecil's vision and political skill. Cecil's son

A portrait of Cecil Calvert, the second Lord Baltimore, handing a map of Maryland to his young grandson Cecil, who was called Cis.

Charles, who was the third Lord Baltimore, lost the Maryland charter during the reign of England's William and Mary, the Protestant king and queen who undid much of what Cecil had fought for.

Under William and Mary, Protestants threw out

the Act of Toleration, closed the towering Catholic church at St. Mary's, and harassed Catholic citizens. In 1695, Protestants moved the colonial capital to the settlement of Anne Arundel Town. (Renamed Annapolis, it is still the capital of Maryland.) The Maryland charter was returned to the Calverts after 24 long years, during which the family had collected land rents but had no influence over the colony's fate. By then, Cecil's grandson held the title of Lord Baltimore.

The Calverts' control spanned most of the 144 years from the founding of Maryland to the Revolutionary War. No other proprietary family in colonial America lasted that long, and it is fair to say that Cecil deserves a great deal of the credit. Yet today, he is not well known, even in the land he founded. Maryland's Cecil County, at the upper end of Chesapeake Bay, is named for him, and the city of Baltimore, Maryland, is named for all the lords Baltimore. Cecil's portrait hangs among other members of the Calvert family in a library in Baltimore. It is the only known original

> *Frederick Calvert, the last Lord Baltimore, was a teenager when he inherited his title and colony in 1751. Other than collecting rents and working out deals for relatives living in Maryland, Frederick had little to do with his colony. As the American colonies moved toward the Revolutionary War, Frederick traveled, squandered his wealth, and got into embarrassing scandals with women.*

painting of Cecil, although there are many modern engravings and illustrations of his likeness. No great statues or monuments were ever built in his honor.

This lack of attention paid to one of America's colonial founders is due, in part, to how little is known about Cecil. He left little evidence of his personality and of his daily life, but his leadership was revolutionary.

Although persecuted for his religion, he made the decision not to shrink away from action. He chose to launch a risky venture in America, and he chose to fight for his rights in England during a time so dangerous that even Charles, the king of England, lost his head to the Puritans. For a short time, Protestants and Catholics and Native Americans in Maryland worked and lived together. Rather than force people to follow a single faith, as the Puritans of New England and the king of England required, Lord Baltimore offered tolerance.

It was far from a perfect system. It was not fair to everyone, especially to the displaced American Indians, to people who were not Christians, and to black people. But long before the American Revolution, Cecil showed it was possible for citizens to be loyal to their country while following different religious faiths. Rather than create a Catholic empire, as his Protestant enemies in Virginia warned he would do, the second Lord Baltimore built an English

Frederick Calvert, the sixth and final Lord Baltimore

community in America where the government did not tell citizens how to worship.

This ability to worship without government control—the separation of church and state—became

By the time of the American Revolution, St. Mary's City had been abandoned and forgotten. It had begun to disappear after the Protestants moved the Maryland capital to Annapolis. In 1934, more than 100,000 people returned to the site to celebrate Maryland's 300th anniversary. The old statehouse was reconstructed for the 1934 celebration. In 1966, the state established a museum on the site. Today the National Historic Landmark includes an active archeology program, 17th-century tobacco plantation, brick church, furnished houses, and an Indian hamlet.

one the most important freedoms in the nation formed by the Revolutionary War. The framers of the U.S. Constitution made sure to include the freedom of religion as a central element of American democracy. In this respect, Cecil Calvert was ahead of his time.

In Maryland today, people are working to discover more about the first colonists. Visitors to Maryland's Chesapeake shore can take a short boat ride to St. Clement's Island, now a state park, where Leonard Calvert and the original Marylanders touched ground in 1634. Each year, local actors dressed like the original colonists land on St. Clement's Island and read aloud Cecil Calvert's famous instructions to settlers. Not far away, Historic St. Mary's City is being researched and reconstructed as it appeared in the 1600s.

For centuries, Cecil Calvert rested in an unmarked grave in London, but he finally got a tombstone. In 1996, the tall ship *Pride of Baltimore II* sailed from

St. Mary's City to England, the reverse journey of the *Ark* and *Dove*. The ship carried a 250-pound (113-kilogram) memorial stone, a gift from the citizens of Maryland to their founder, Cecil Calvert, Lord Baltimore. The stone was placed at St. Giles-in-the-Field Church in Middlesex, where Cecil lay buried. Lord Baltimore never had the chance to come to America, but almost 400 years after his birth, America came to him. ✐

A historical marker at the site of Maryland's first statehouse

LORD BALTIMORE'S LIFE

1625

His father is made Lord Baltimore and given a 2,300-acre (920-hectare) estate in Ireland, and resigns his position as secretary of state

1605

Born on August 8 to George Calvert and Anne Mynne

1600

1620

1611

The King James Bible, commissioned by the British king, is published

1620

The *Mayflower* with its Pilgrim passengers sails from England to North America

WORLD EVENTS

1627

Left in charge of
family estates while
his father travels
to Avalon Colony
in Newfoundland,
Canada; marries Anne
Arundell (c. 1627)

1629

His father asks King
Charles to grant him
a section of land
that becomes the
Maryland Colony

1628

John Bunyan,
popular English
religious author,
is born

1629

Empress Meisho
ascends to the throne
of Japan

Life and Times

LORD BALTIMORE'S LIFE

1632

Gains the title of Lord Baltimore after his father's death; accepts Maryland Charter granted to Calvert family by King Charles

1633

Sends off his first 140 Maryland settlers aboard the *Ark* and *Dove* with his colonization plan

1634

His settlers establish colonial capital at St. Mary's

1630

1633

Galileo Gallilei, on trial before the Inquisition in Rome, is forced to recant his sun-centered view of the solar system

1634

Jean Nicolet lands at Green Bay and explores Wisconsin

WORLD EVENTS

1638

Consents to Maryland Assembly demand for more power to govern the colony

1645

Remains idle in England while Richard Ingle controls Maryland Colony during England's civil war

1640

1636

Harvard College founded at Cambridge, Massachusetts

1638

Louis XIV, future King of France, is born

1642

Isaac Newton, English mathematician and philosopher, is born

LORD BALTIMORE'S LIFE

1661

Installs his son, Charles Calvert, as governor of the Maryland Colony

1649

His Act of Toleration ensures equal rights for Maryland's Catholics and Protestants

1655

1649

King Charles I of England is overthrown by radical Protestants and beheaded

1655

Christian Huggens discovers the rings of Saturn

WORLD EVENTS

1667

His colony's capital is incorporated as St. Mary's City

1675

Dies in England at age 70

1675

1670

The Hudson's Bay Company is founded

1681

The Canal du Midi, a 150-mile (240-km) long canal in southern France, is finished after eight years of work

DATE OF BIRTH: August 8, 1605

PLACE OF BIRTH: Kent, England

FATHER: Sir George Calvert
(c. 1578–1632)

MOTHER: Anne Mynne (1578–1622)

EDUCATION: Attended Trinity College,
Oxford

SPOUSE: Lady Anne Arundell
(c. 1615–1649)

DATE OF MARRIAGE: c. 1628

CHILDREN: George (1634–1636)
Charles (1637–1714)
Anne Calvert
Mary Calvert (1630–1663)
Elizabeth Calvert

DATE OF DEATH: November 30, 1675

PLACE OF BURIAL: Middlesex, England

IN THE LIBRARY

Collier, Christopher, and James Lincoln Collier. *Clash of Cultures: Prehistory–1638.* New York: Benchmark Books, 1998.

Jensen, Ann. *Leonard Calvert and the Maryland Adventure.* Centreville, Md.: Tidewater Publications, 1998.

Lough, Loree. *Lord Baltimore: English Politician and Colonist.* Philadelphia: Chelsea House Publishers, 2000.

Wiener, Roberta, and James R. Arnold. *Maryland: The History of the Colony.* Chicago: Raintree, 2005.

LOOK FOR MORE SIGNATURE LIVES BOOKS ABOUT THIS ERA:

Anne Hutchinson: *Puritan Protester*
ISBN 0-7565-1577-7

William Penn: *Founder of Pennsylvania*
ISBN 0-7565-1598-X

Roger Williams: *Founder of Rhode Island*
ISBN 0-7565-1596-3

John Winthrop: *First Governor of Massachusetts*
ISBN 0-7565-1591-2

On the Web

For more information on *Lord Baltimore*, use FactHound.

1. Go to *www.facthound.com*
2. Type in a search word related to this book or this book ID: 0756515920
3. Click on the *Fetch It* button.

FactHound will fetch the best Web sites for you.

Historic Sites

Historic St. Mary's
18559 Hogaboom Lane
St. Mary's City, MD
240/895-4990
The reconstructed 17th-century village where Lord Baltimore's first settlers founded Maryland in 1634

Enoch Pratt Free Library
400 Cathedral St.
Baltimore, MD
410/396-5430
A library holding original paintings of all six lords Baltimore and featuring student exhibits, programs, and events

baron
a knighted member of the British ruling class

indentured servants
people who work for someone else for a certain
period of time in return for payment of travel and
living costs

manor
a large estate of at least 1,000 acres (400 hectares)
where the owner had special privileges and rights

monarchy
a type of government in which a king or queen is
the head of state

palatinate
a system of owning land where a hereditary landlord manages a huge piece of land

patron
a person named as a guardian or supporter

pinnace
a light sailing ship that could be used to navigate
shallow rivers

predecessor
a person who has previously held a position
or office

proprietary
someone who holds exclusive rights to something
or is granted ownership of a colony

quitrent
a fixed rent payable to a colony's leader

tolerance
having sympathy for beliefs different from
your own

Chapter 1

Page 12, line 17: Andrew White, S.J. *Voyage to Maryland (1633)/ Relatio Itineris in Marilandiam*, translated from Latin and edited by Barbara Lawatsch-Boomgarden with Josef Ijsewijn. Waucond, Illinois: Blchazy-Carducci Publishers, 1995, p. 26.

Page 13, line 22: Ibid., p. 32.

Chapter 2

Page 22, line 6: John D. Krugler. *English and Catholic: The Lords of Baltimore and the Seventeenth Century*. Baltimore: Johns Hopkins University Press, 2004, p. 70.

Chapter 3

Page 32, sidebar: The Maryland Charter.

Page 32, line 28: "Leonard Calvert: First Governor of Maryland." 5 Dec. 2005. www.co.saint marys.md.us/recreate/museums/leonardcalvert.asp.

Page 33, line 28: *The Calvert Papers*. Baltimore: J. Murphy & Co., 1889, p. 134.

Page 36, line 15: Rev. Edward D. Neill. *The Founders of Maryland as Portrayed in Manuscripts, Provincial Records and Early Documents*. Albany, N.Y.: Joel Munsell, 1876, p. 63.

Chapter 4

Page 40, line 5: W. Stitt Robinson. "Conflicting Views on Landholding: Lord Baltimore and the Experiences of Colonial Maryland with Native Americans." *Maryland Historical Magazine*, Vol. 83, Summer 1988, p. 86.

Chapter 5

Page 50, line 9: *Voyage to Maryland*, p. 35.

Page 52, line 9: Ibid., p. 39.

Page 53, line 1: Robert Brugger. *Maryland: A Middle Temperament, 1634-1980*. Baltimore: Johns Hopkins University Press, 1988, p. 3.

Page 53, line 6: Nan Hayden Agle, and Frances Atchinson Bacon. *The Lords Baltimore*, New York: Holt, Rinehart & Winston, 1967, p. 66.

Chapter 8

Page 75, line 7: King James I. "A Counterblaste to Tobacco, 1604," 5 Dec. 2005. www.tobacco.org/resources/history/ Tobacco_History17.html.

Chapter 9

Page 85, line 9: *The Calvert Papers*, p. 285.

Page 85, line 10: Ibid.

Page 86, line 1: Ibid.

Agle, Nan Hayden, and Frances Atchinson Bacon. *The Lords Baltimore.* New York: Holt, Rinehart & Winston, 1967.

Bozman, John Leeds. *A Sketch of the History of Maryland during the Three First Years after Its Settlement.* Baltimore: Edward J. Coale, 1811.

Browne, William Hand, ed. *Proceedings of the Council of Maryland, 1636–1667.* Baltimore: Maryland Historical Society, 1885.

Brugger, Robert J. *Maryland: A Middle Temperament 1634-1980.* Baltimore: Johns Hopkins University Press, 1988.

Dozer, Donald Marquand. *Portrait of the Free State: A History of Maryland.* Cambridge, Md.: Tidewater Publishers, 1976.

Foster, James W. *George Calvert: The Early Years.* Baltimore: Maryland Historical Society, 1983.

Krugler, John D. *English and Catholic: The Lords of Baltimore and the Seventeenth Century.* Baltimore: Johns Hopkins University Press, 2004.

Manakee, Harold R. *Indians of Early Maryland.* Baltimore: Maryland Historical Society, 1959.

Neill, Rev. Edward D. *The Founders of Maryland as Portrayed in Manuscripts, Provincial Records and Early Documents.* Albany, N.Y.: Joel Munsell, 1876.

Papenfuse, Edward C., and Joseph M. Coale III. *The Maryland State Archives Atlas of Maps of Maryland 1608–1908.* Baltimore: Johns Hopkins University Press, 2003.

Riordan, Timothy B. *The Plundering Time: Maryland and the English Civil War 1645–1646.* Baltimore: Maryland Historical Society, 2004.

White, Andrew, S.J. *Voyage to Maryland (1633)/Relatio Itineris in Marilandiam,* translated from Latin and edited by Barbara Lawatsch-Boomgarden with Josef Ijsewijn. Waucond, Illinois: Blchazy-Carducci Publishers, 1995.

Wilson, William E. "Maryland Their Maryland." *American Heritage Magazine,* August 1967.

J. Dennis Robinson is editor and owner of the popular New England Web site *SeacoastNH.com*. A lecturer, freelance journalist, and media scriptwriter, he is the author of a number of books about history. He lives near the Piscataqua River in Portsmouth, New Hampshire, with his wife Maryellen.

Image Credits